GREATNESS

For Kids

A Guide to Achieving Dreams

Written by Sebashten Kidd, U.S.A.

Illustrated by Evgenija Burchak, Ukraine

Produced by SAKS Publishing, U.S.A.

Copyright © 2022 by SAKS Publishing in the U.S.A.

All rights reserved. This book or any portion thereof may not be reproduced or used in any manner without the permission of the publisher except for the use of brief quotations in a book review.

It is a pleasure to present you with this guide to help you discover your greatness inside.

INSTRUCTIONS	1
DREAM BANK	3
CHAPTER 1 BEGINNING YOUR JOURNEY	6
CHAPTER 2 DEVELOPING A PLAN	18
CHAPTER 3 OVERCOMING CHALLENGES	28
CHAPTER 4 ACHIEVING YOUR DREAM	40

INSTRUCTIONS

Greatness For Kids is your guide to achieving your dreams. There are 4 chapters. In each chapter there are activities for you to complete. When finished with all activities, you will have created a Dream Map for one of your dreams.

A Dream Map is like a treasure map. It leads you towards your dream and keeps you focused on making it real. Below is an example of a Dream Map. The dream is to Paint Oil Paintings. You will see the steps taken to create this Dream Map as you read.

PAINT OIL PAINTINGS

I love to design and create things.

I will be the greatest Painter!

I can paint with acrylics. I can draw. I am a fast learner. I am creative. I am patient.

I Have AMAZING ABILITIES

1. Watch videos of famous oil painters to learn techniques.
2. Learn how to mix colors.
3. Save money to buy supplies.
4. Paint a mountain with trees and a pond.
5. Paint an abstract painting.
6. Paint a MASTERPIECE!

To create your Dream Map, you will need:

- ★ a sheet of paper
- ★ a pencil
- ★ an eraser
- ★ markers
- ★ crayons
- ★ colored pencils

You will also need a dream.
So... let's begin.

ACTIVITY 1: Select a challenging dream you would like to achieve in the next few months, or within the next year. Write it at the top of your map with pencil. Then color your dream any way you wish. Visit the DREAM BANK for ideas.

PAINT OIL PAINTINGS

DREAM

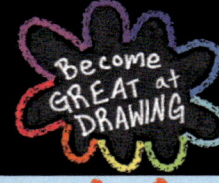

- Play the ELECTRIC GUITAR
- Play TENNIS
- Become GREAT at DRAWING
- Create MUSIC VIDEOS
- Run a Race
- Become Great at Computers
- Design Clothes
- Film a Movie
- Catch a Fish
- Collect Coins
- Write a Song
- Learn to Surf
- Play Football
- Grow Fruits and Vegetables
- Design an App
- Hit a Home Run
- Create a Puppet Show
- Code Software
- Learn A New Language
- Climb a Mountain
- Bake Desserts
- Play Music
- Build a Train Set
- Build Model Airplanes
- Become a Leader
- Collect Model Cars
- Start a Club
- Make Candles
- Act in a Play
- Raise Ladybugs
- Get a Black Belt in Martial Arts
- Build a Flower Garden
- Create an Art Studio
- Start a Band
- Play a Song on the Violin
- Save Money
- Play Golf
- Make Pottery
- Learn Photography
- Play Hockey
- Read Faster
- Build more Strength
- Win a Spelling Bee
- Create a Cartoon
- Learn to Knit and Sew
- Win a Dance Competition
- Build a Bike
- Play the Piano
- Build a Robot
- Play Soccer
- Design Jewelry
- Become Great at Math
- Do A Research Project

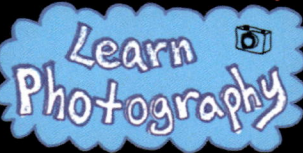

BANK 🏛 Write a BOOK

- Improve At Gymnastics
- Win a Video Game Contest
- Write my Life Story
- Learn to Play a Flute
- Win A Chess Tournament
- Build An Aquarium
- Build A Science Lab
- Sketch A Comic
- Start a Business
- Build A Clubhouse
- Make A Fruit Salad
- Do Tricks on a Skateboard
- Paint Oil Paintings
- Create A Game
- Become Great at Sudoku
- Get Organized
- Cook Meals
- Develop My Talents
- Complete A Hard Puzzle
- Make The Honor Roll
- Build A Birdhouse
- Raise A Snake
- Volunteer in my Community
- Start A YouTube Channel
- Bake Bread
- Design Flower Bouquets
- Improve at Swimming
- Make Candy
- Write Poetry
- Stitch A Quilt
- Explore Astronomy
- Shoot 3-Pointers in Basketball
- Learn Origami
- Become A Magician
- Adopt a Puppy
- Build More Friendships
- Collect Insects
- Throw A Party
- Create A Wooden Sculpture
- Play Cricket
- Create An Engineering Experiment
- Learn to DJ Music
- Become A Cheerleader
- Learn Backgammon
- Improve my Health
- Create Advertising Videos
- Start A Fashion Show
- Learn about the Stock Market
- Build A Table
- Win an Art contest
- Build my Confidence
- Play Drums
- Raise A Hamster

4

When you have completed Activity 1,
you will be ready to continue with Chapter 1 of

GREATNESS For Kids.

PAINT OIL PAINTINGS

5

CHAPTER 1
BEGINNING YOUR JOURNEY

Life is a journey
of reaching for your dreams,
taking you up tall mountains
and down rivers and streams.

But how do you make
your dreams become real,
so you have something
you can touch and feel?

When you strive for greatness
in everything you do,
your biggest wishes
will begin to come true.

strive: to try to get, or do, something

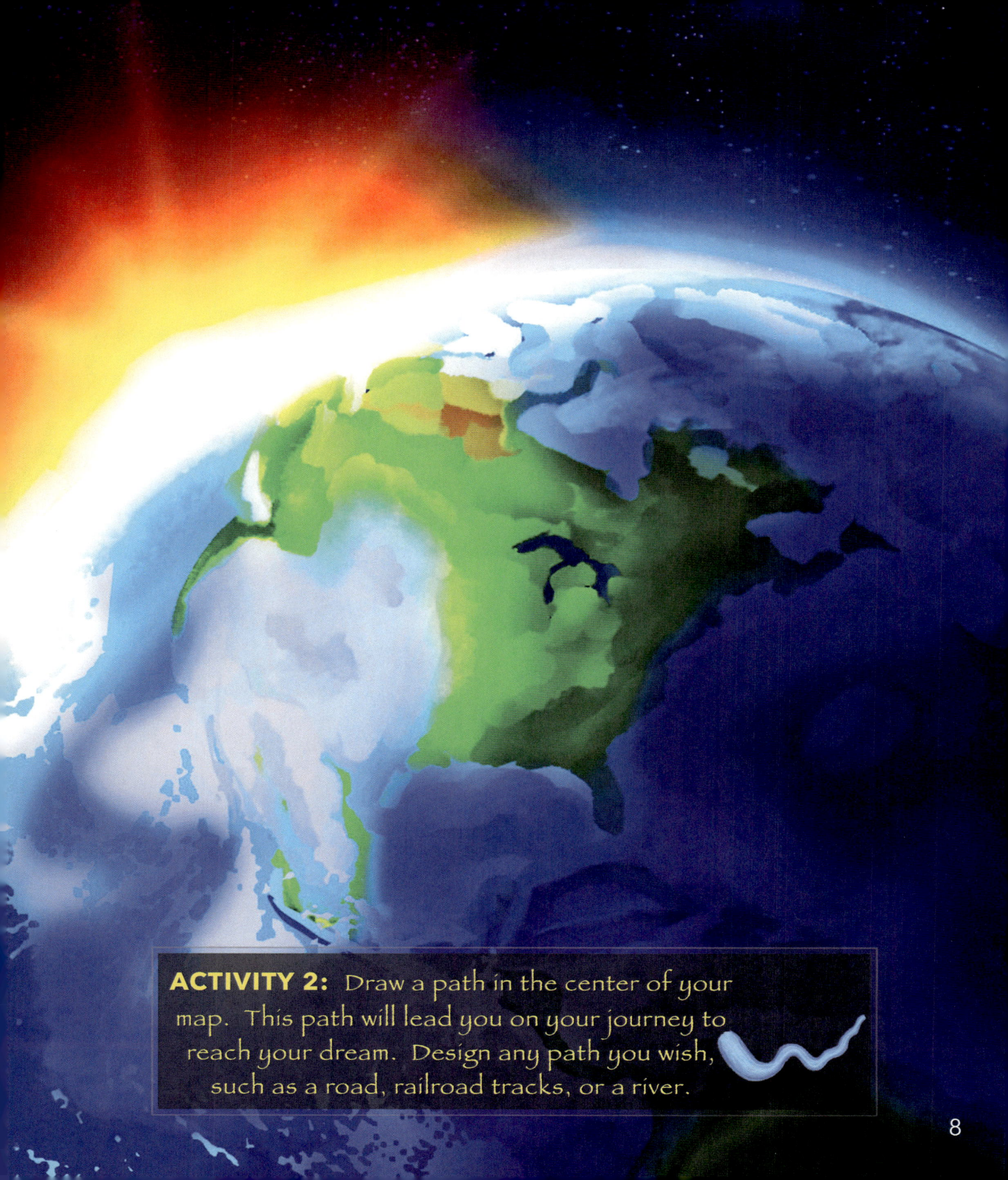

ACTIVITY 2: Draw a path in the center of your map. This path will lead you on your journey to reach your dream. Design any path you wish, such as a road, railroad tracks, or a river.

Right now you have
greatness within
that is starting to grow.
Greatness that will lead you
towards hidden treasures,
like diamonds in a volcano.

Your greatness will
slowly uncover as you
perform your best,
and work your hardest
to reach high levels of success.

As you find what makes you great
and continue to improve,
you will become hot like lava
and ready to move.

ACTIVITY 3: Draw a treasure chest full of treasure in the top-left corner of your map. The treasure is the greatness within you that will be uncovered as you make your dream come to life.

To discover your greatness
and watch it glow, ...

.... release your energy
and let it flow.

Let your <u>enthusiasm</u> burst and gush out.
Be ready to show the world
what you are all about.

<u>enthusiasm</u>: to show lots of interest and excitement

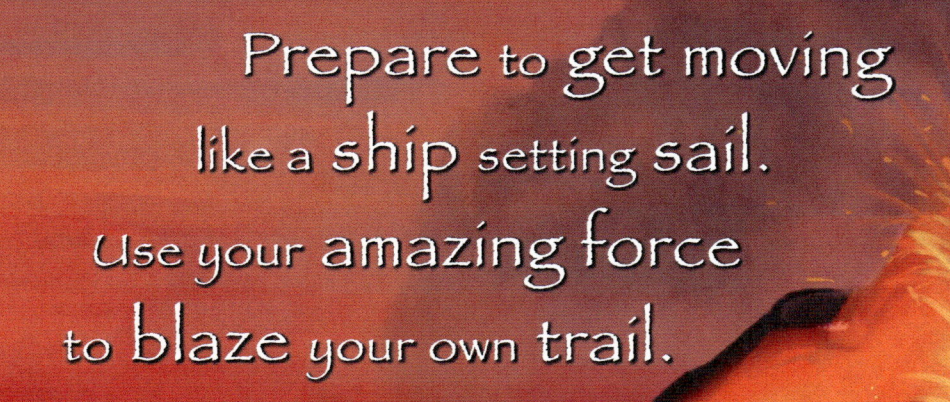

Prepare to get moving
like a ship setting sail.
Use your amazing force
to blaze your own trail.

Achieving
greatness
is what you were
born to do, and it all
begins with one person,
and that is you.

ACTIVITY 4: Draw the sun at the beginning of your path to give you the boost of energy you need to begin your journey.

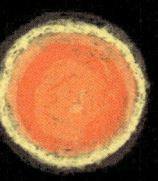

12

You are a
<u>unique</u> individual,
like a moose roaming Planet Earth,
in search of great adventures
and new dreams to give birth.

Dreams come in sizes big and small,
and each has a purpose
to help you stand tall.

ACTIVITY 5: Draw an image of your dream at the end of your path to help you stay focused on what you want.

<u>unique</u>: something that is different, or special

To begin your journey towards the dreams you wish to achieve, ...

... have courage

and use your powers inside to believe.

You can do anything
that can be imagined in your heart
when you are <u>confident</u>
and have the courage to
move forward
and start.

Be brave
and go after every dream,
no matter how difficult
they may seem.

<u>confident</u>: to have a strong belief in yourself

Believe in **yourself** and your abilities and you will soar like an eagle towards endless possibilities.

ACTIVITY 6: Draw a mountain near your path to give you confidence and courage along the way. Write a statement around your mountain to show your confidence.

When you have completed Activities 1 thru 6,
you will be ready to continue with Chapter 2 of

GREATNESS For Kids.

PAINT OIL PAINTINGS

I will be the greatest Painter!

CHAPTER 2
DEVELOPING A PLAN

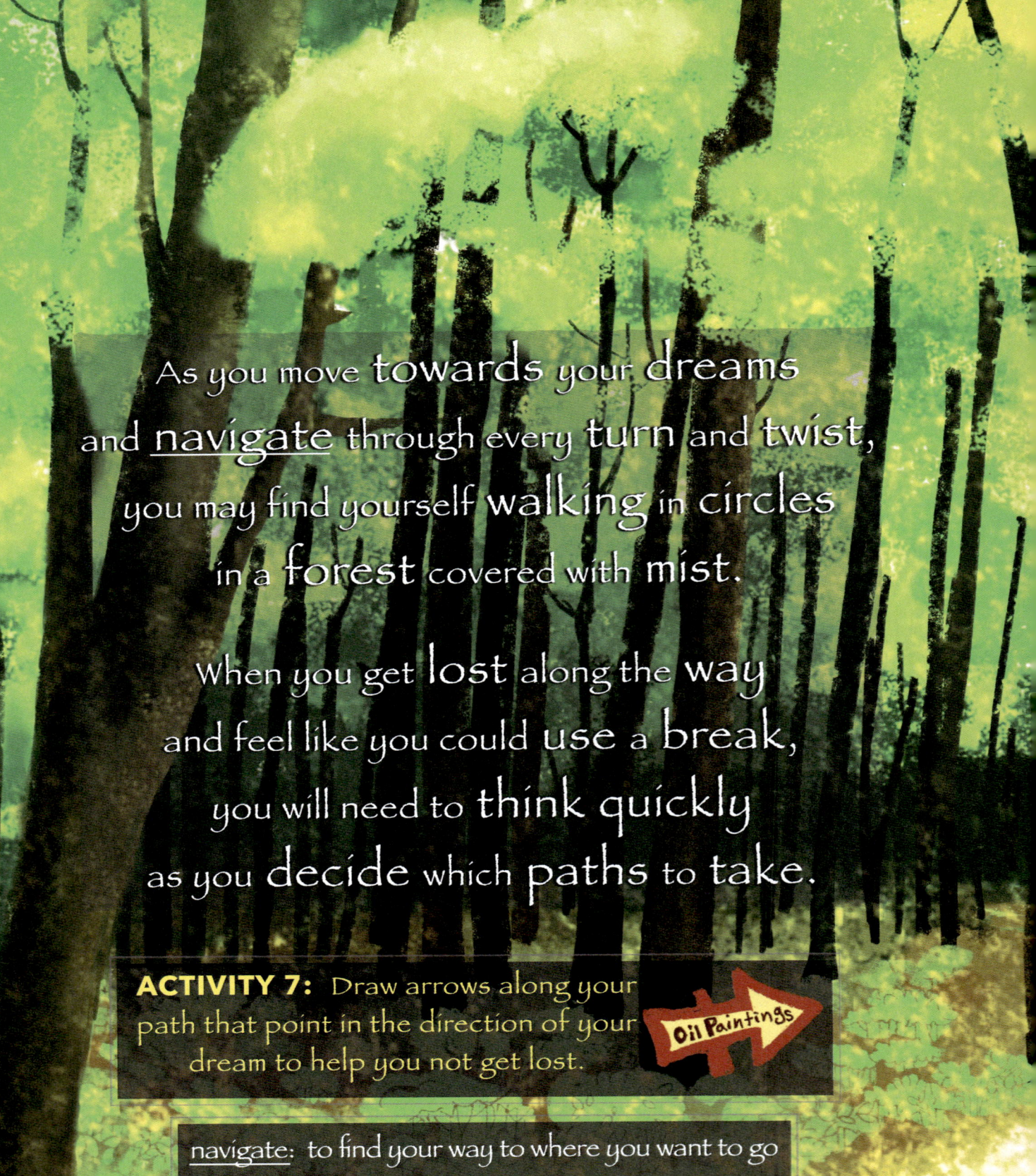

As you move towards your dreams
and navigate through every turn and twist,
you may find yourself walking in circles
in a forest covered with mist.

When you get lost along the way
and feel like you could use a break,
you will need to think quickly
as you decide which paths to take.

ACTIVITY 7: Draw arrows along your path that point in the direction of your dream to help you not get lost.

Oil Paintings

navigate: to find your way to where you want to go

Some paths will be short.
Some paths will be long.
Each path will lead you to places
that help your confidence grow strong.

When there are several paths ahead
for you to choose, ...

...follow your passions

and you cannot lose.

Let the things you enjoy
be your guide.
They will take you
on an awesome ride.

Be inspired
to try new things.
It will help you
spread your wings.

Activity 8: Draw a heart near your path. Then write why you are passionate about your dream.

inspired: the feeling to do something special

Think about what excites you the most
when you are faced with a difficult decision.
Follow what you feel in your heart
and it will expand your vision.

Do what you love, love what you do,
and you will be following the passions
inside of you.

If you know what you enjoy
but not sure where to begin,
you may feel trapped in a web,
and your head will spin.

When you get <u>confused</u> and start to fall behind,
focus on your talents
and you will have peace of mind.

<u>confused</u>: when you are not sure what is going on

All the skills and strengths
that come naturally to you
are the talents and gifts
you need to pursue.

Improve your strengths
and make them as sharp as a knife.
Practice new skills
to bring more success into your life.

ACTIVITY 9: Draw a star near your path. Then list the strengths and talents you have now that can help make your dream easier to accomplish.

And when you still feel stuck in the woods
surrounded by trees,
and the weeds
are high above your knees, ...

pursue: to go after, or chase, something

...set goals
and life will become a breeze.

Goals are targets you aim to achieve
to get the rewards you wish to receive.

Each goal becomes part of a plan you create
to attract what you want, like bait.

Goals tell you what actions to take,
and when they need to be complete.
And each goal must be challenging
to make you want to fly out of your seat.

Setting goals is a process
that you must continue to repeat.
And as you reach each goal
you will dance to a new beat.

ACTIVITY 10: Draw a target in the bottom-left corner of your map. Then list 3 or more goals that you must achieve to make your dream become real.

When you have completed Activities 1 thru 10,
you will be ready to continue with Chapter 3 of

GREATNESS For Kids.

PAINT OIL PAINTINGS

I love to design and create things.
I will be the greatest Painter!
I can paint with acrylics.
I can draw.
I am patient.
I am creative.
I am a fast learner.

1. **Watch videos** of famous oil painters to learn techniques.
2. **Learn how** to mix colors.
3. **Save money** to buy supplies.
4. **Paint** a mountain with trees and a pond.
5. **Paint** an abstract painting.
6. **Paint** a MASTERPIECE!

CHAPTER 3
OVERCOMING CHALLENGES

At times, the goals you set
will take you on a long journey,
where you will make mistakes
and be going nowhere
in a hurry.

You might feel like a camel in the desert
with no end in sight,
and your energy will go down
as you begin to lose
daylight.

When you are far away from
reaching your destination,
think positively ...

<u>destination</u>: the place you are traveling to

... and have motivation.

Be strong when the sand is blowing in your face.
Put one foot in front of the other
and stay in the race.

When life makes you huff and puff,
dig your heels in
and be tough.

ACTIVITY 11: Draw animal footprints along your path leading towards your dream to motivate you to move forward when you make mistakes.

And when you get tired and need a vacation,
stay motivated, ...

...and use your
imagination.

You have an incredible imagination.
It gives you the wonderful powers of creation.

Your imagination creates pictures in bright bold colors,
helping you get through the dry, hot summers.

Whether you are melting from heat or freezing like ice, use your imagination and pretend you are roaming through paradise.

Relax your mind and keep dreaming your dreams like a sleeping seal, and someday soon your dreams will become real.

ACTIVITY 12: Draw an island in the bottom-right corner of your map to give you a place where you can relax and imagine your dream coming to life.

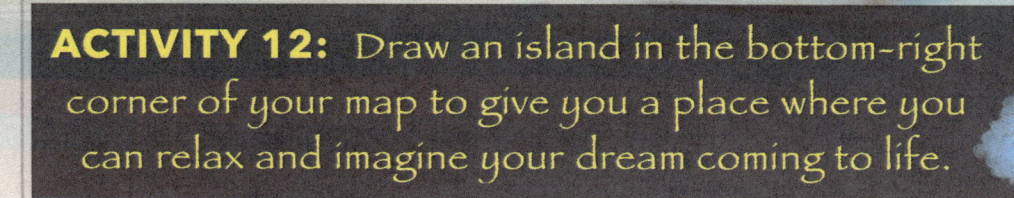

paradise: a beautiful and happy place

Your imagination will take you to a place of fantasy, where your mind can wander off into a far away galaxy.

You will see colors you have never seen before, that will make you curious and wanting to learn more.

ACTIVITY 13: Write a positive message on your map to inspire you to accomplish your dream. Use words that describe the universe in your message, such as:

MAGNIFICENT   BRILLIANT   INCREDIBLE   DAZZLE
SHIMMERING   AWESOME   VIVID   SPARKLE   SHINE

I Have AMAZING ABILITIES

But life will not always be
so clear and so bright.
You will face many barriers
that will block the bright light.

barriers: things that get in your way

There will be tasks you need to perform
that make you feel afraid,
like you will fail.

There will be answers you fear you may not know
that will make you
want to yell.

You try to leave your worries behind,
but they continue to
cross your mind.

ACTIVITY 14: Draw fish in a fishbowl anywhere on your map to give you something fun to focus on to help take your worries away.

When life gets scary
and brings you to tears, ...

.... rise up and conquer your fears.

Hold your head high in the sky
when challenges come up in your face.
Be courageous and don't give them space.

When the thoughts in your mind give you
a frightening emotion,
overcome your fears
and send them deep into the ocean.

conquer: to defeat a challenge

Live your life confidently
and soon you will see
that the fears you have feared the most
are not as fearful as you thought they would be.

ACTIVITY 15: Draw sharks near your path. The sharks are the fears you will face on your journey.

PAINT OIL PAINTINGS

I love to design and create things.

I will be the greatest Painter!

Oil Paintings

I can draw. I am patient. I am creative. I am a fast learner. I can paint with acrylics.

I Have AMAZING ABILITIES

1. Watch videos of famous oil painters to learn techniques.
2. Learn how to mix colors.
3. Save money to buy supplies.
4. Paint a mountain with trees and a pond.
5. Paint an abstract painting.
6. Paint a MASTERPIECE!

CHAPTER 4
ACHIEVING YOUR DREAM

But no matter how much you
hope and wish
for your dreams to occur,
new obstacles will continue to
enter your life
and cause your vision to blur.

You will look up
and notice the sky above
is no longer blue,
and before you know it
the storm has come
towards you.

ACTIVITY 16: Draw a storm near the center of your path. The storm is any challenge you will have on your journey. Suggestions of storms are:

BLIZZARD   HURRICANE   RAINSTORM   TORNADO

When a <u>disturbance</u>
comes your way
and you cannot see clear,
stay calm, be patient ...

<u>disturbance</u>: something that gets in the way of a quiet, peaceful moment

… and persevere.

Soar above your troubles
and view them from up high,
like an eagle looking down on the clouds
drifting up in the sky.

persevere: to continue moving forward during a challenge

Anytime you feel like
it may be time to quit,
have perseverance
and fight with all of your grit.

And if the world around
gives you little joy and cheer,
ride the lightning through the storm
until you see your victory appear.

ACTIVITY 17: Draw eagles flying around your map to help you defeat your challenges.

Then after the storm has passed
and your vision becomes clear, …

grit: to be strong when facing a difficulty

...seek every opportunity

that is in front of you and near.

Press forward with blazing speed
towards what you are wishing for
in your heart.

Follow your instincts
and aim for new opportunities
like a target to a dart.

ACTIVITY 18: Draw tiger eyes near the end of your path to help you find new dreams to go after as you get close to making this dream real.

opportunity: the chance to do something new

instincts: following your heart and mind when trying to make good decisions

45

Be determined and believe you will succeed in the opportunities you pursue...

determined: to go after what you want

46

... and you will begin to
unleash the
greatness
within you.

unleash: to release something

47

ACTIVITY 19: Draw a trophy at the end of your path. The trophy is your reward for attempting to achieve your dream.

48

You have achieved so much
in such a short time,
but there are many more mountains
for you to climb.

There are new worlds to explore
with more to see,
and they will all become a part
of who you wish to be.

Focus on your accomplishments
and performing your best,
and you will make your dreams become real
and discover your greatness.

ACTIVITY 20: Make your final edits to your Dream Map. Then add a border. Add additional images if you wish, such as a car for a road, a train for train tracks, or a boat for a river.

50

PAINT OIL PAINTINGS

When you have completed Activities 1 thru 20, you will have completed your Dream Map. And you will be ready to begin pursuing your dream, and discovering your greatness.

1. Watch videos of famous oil painters to learn techniques.
2. Learn how to mix colors.
3. Save money to buy supplies.
4. Paint a mountain with trees and a pond.
5. Paint an abstract painting.
6. Paint a MASTERPIECE!

Have Amazing Abilities

I love to design and create things.

I will be the greatest painter!

I am a fast learner.
I can paint with acrylics.
I can draw.
I am patient.
I am creative.

Made in the USA
Columbia, SC
28 April 2022